All of These Feelings

Lauran Hirschi

BookLeaf Publishing

India | USA | UK

All of These Feelings © 2024 Lauran
Hirschi

All rights reserved.

No part of this publication may be
reproduced, stored in a retrieval system, or
transmitted, in any form or by any means,
electronic, mechanical, photocopying,
recording or otherwise, without the prior
written permission of the presenters.

Lauran Hirschi asserts the moral right to be
identified as author of this work.

Presentation by *BookLeaf Publishing*

Web: www.bookleafpub.com

E-mail: info@bookleafpub.com

ISBN: 9789363307223

First edition 2024

*For Patricia and Carol. If my mind is a garden,
the lilacs are blooming there because of you
two.*

ACKNOWLEDGEMENT

To my family and friends who haven't been scared away by my overactive tear ducts or emotional rambling. Thanks for listening to my words and boosting my confidence in my writing. I would not be here without all of you! Special thanks to some of my dear friends who saw the good in my writing even when I struggled to do so. This includes (but is not limited to) Andy, Bonnie, Carol-Lynne, Chris, Claire, Erika, Heather, Joe, Kelsea, Krista, Meghan, Monai, Tara, and Val.

PREFACE

For as long as I have been able to write, I have been making lists and writing things out. In middle school and high school I remember writing some of my first poems. This practice continued until the present day, and I often process through writing my thoughts and feelings out in short paragraphs.

I have often described myself in the past as an "emotional being," but the older I get the more I shake my head at that description. I think all humans are emotional. My feelings just have a tendency to be expressed a bit loudly. This, as you will likely see within the pages of this book, is something that I have not always had the easiest time dealing with. However, the more I grow and interact with people whose stories look differently than mine, the more I think that having these unique modes of feeling can be instructive rather than destructive.

Lost Looking Up

I often get caught with my eyes in the clouds;
My inner child longing to jump
Headlong into the fluffiest ones.
I lose myself in their colors-
At dawn, at sunset, after a storm-
The shades of blue, purple, pink, and orange,
And in the midst of a downpour
When the sun breaks through
And paints a rainbow
Across the horizontal haze.
A sky will stay with me for days.
My camera roll is filled with snapshots of those
skies
And behind my eyelids the views reprise, filled
with emotion, wrapped up in awe
How grateful I am to bear witness to
Each spring reawakening, each winter thaw.
Even the greyest, dullest of views
Takes up that all-encompassing space, and
eventually moves on.
And I've been on enough plane rides to know,
There's always a higher plane you can go to
To look at the smothering, silvery sheet
As it's own kind of beauty, full and complete.
Often I have to elevate my gaze,

To look past the world with its messes and
mazes,
And gaining perspective that though I may fall,
How lucky I am to have flown so high at all.

Enough

I might always be
too much for some,
too little for others--
But when will I let myself
Be enough
for just me?

Directionless

Two paths split in the woods-
and I can't decide between them.
So I run headlong
Right down the middle of where they diverge..
and now I'm lost,
with thorns in my feet and
brambles is my hair,
Wondering how I got so far off course.

Yet when I worry less about the other trails,
My eyes see instead what lies ahead.
And I wander, eager and longing,
To see each unique beauty
Along the winding path I've made for myself.
There's so much I lose sight of
In looking everywhere but right in front me.
As I focus in on what is directly in view,
I'll know better where to next place my foot-
Instead of trying to guess
What someone else would do.

The Switch

I woke up this morning
With a tightness in my chest,
And three seconds into the day
Was feeling less than my best.

And now, laying here
At the close of the night,
My breaths come much easier,
I genuinely feel alright.

When did it switch?
Did I make one decision
That got me on track
Instead of trapped by self-derision?

Or was it instead
In the small, even breaths
And thoughts of, "I'm in control,
Not out of my depth."

It is an adage oft repeated
But maybe not enough felt,
That little actions can change
What we do with what we are dealt.

Living with a Swollen Heart, Lesson 1

So you've got big emotions,
here's where to start:
Remember they don't have to tear you apart.

Accept your tears, do not hold them back.
Excitement and fear can be confused as heart
attacks.

There will be those who shy away from the
depths of your sentimentality,
Remember that you do not feel for them.

When the world seems too heavy,
And you feel you are coming undone,
Become instead a flower whose sole purpose is
to bask in the sun.

Focus on your breath.
As outside anxieties converge on your petals,
Picture yourself as the stem.

Connecting back to your roots
You have power to choose
How to live with your swollen heart.

Backpedal

You know when you are little
And learning to ride a bike?
There's this nifty trick
Where you can slam your pedal back
And suddenly screech to a halt.

But I remember one day
Riding a set of more "adult" wheels
And as I pushed the pedals backward
All I heard was the chain click a little
But I didn't stop.

Sometimes growing up feels like that.

Like I pedaled up a big hill
But didn't check what kind of
Brakes my bike had.

Like I said yes to something
Before I knew what I really wanted
And now I'm moving too fast.

Careening down
With no pedals to slam back,
No hand brakes,

Too scared to throw my feet down
And stop this spiral of mistakes.

8

Embrace

Embrace the parts of you
That you used to look at and sigh,
Or avoided looking at completely
Because they made you want to cry.

Stop trying to shove yourself
Into itty bitty boxes
Or shut away certain parts
Behind bolts and locks.

Open up.
Stretch out wide.
Let yourself breathe,
No more need to hide.

Maybe everything you were searching for-
Chasing in others, desperate to find-
Has been inside you all along,
You just had to see with eyes more kind.

Suddenly,
You've struck gold.
You ARE gold.
Bold, brave, beautiful, and bright.
Lean into your light.
And embrace it.

The Tide Goes Out

Melancholy waves wash over me,
Crash against the shore of my ordinary day,
"What if's, why's, and how could they's"
Pull me under.

Underprepared and tumbling beneath
The wondering, I chase
Understanding that will never come,
Answers I will never receive.

When you don't know when goodbye was or will
be,
It can be a challenge to fully grieve.
Somewhere deep in my bones
I try to believe
That I am not the sole reason
Everyone decides to leave.

Housekeeping

I resist cleaning my room
Because I am scared
That in the clarity of cleanliness,
My mental junk will stand
More readily on display
And I will have to face myself
In the sparkling mirror and say,
"I have told you for years
That you're not worth the effort.
All the while something inside
whispered to me that that was a lie.
And the divine in me
Pulled and tugged and begged
Me to gaze anew--
But I refused to relent in
My self-hatred
And that is what got me here."
But as I begin to confront it,
As I start pulling down the cobwebs,
In my room and in my mind,
What I find is not so much resistance.
But a small broken soul
In need of love, and a scrub,
But somehow still beautiful
For all she's been snubbed.

And she looks up at me,
In that freshly shined mirror,
Not with anger
Or malice
Or resentment.
She looks at me with
A fear I recognize too well.
"Who sent you?
Can I trust you?
Do you really care?"
Her whisper is so soft,
It's barely even there.
And I realize that I need
To rebuild our trust--
Since it was I that
Bruised and battered her
Because I thought I must.
Something long ago,
Its origins unclear,
Told me I could not
Be good or pretty or fair.
So I broke myself down,
Again and again,
And now I have to choose
To see in these broken pieces
A work of art
Just waiting
To be re-formed.

Checkpoints

"Once I get there I'll be happy,"
You say of some distant achievement
Down the road. Far from here,
Everything will be more clear
After accolades and laud
Ring loud in your ears.

But what of the quiet moments
Before and after the finish line?
What of the times you wanted to throw the towel
in,
But you chose to keep trying?

What of the silent victory?
Of setting the goal in the first place?
Of reaching for something more than
The comfort of a "regular" life,
And finding a new adventure to face?

Each move along the way was made by you--
Even the steps that felt like setbacks, too.

So don't wait to celebrate the victory,
Find it all along the journey.

Courting the Cold

Winter, that ominous stretch of death and darkness. A pale light looms just over the horizon of a frigid day, and I fall into mourning for other times.

Compared with this, the other three seasons appear full of life and light-- even autumn, with its loss of leaves, abounds with change and color.

But something remains on the quiet rocks, a growing I am often too harried to observe. What does winter give birth to? Only rest, stillness, silence?

Even as I write this line, a bird chitters in the trees surrounding me.. almost as if to say, "I am still here, I have not died!"

Indignant, the wind blows over the wood and awakens the leaves. Mother Earth stirs, reminding me her slumber is not eternal, and yet we all need sleep.

Yes, maybe winter is softer-spoken. Maybe I
have to lean in and pay more attention to what
she is trying to tell me.

I do not need to panic if she seems slow to reply
to my wondering and wandering. Sometimes I
am drunk in words- quick retorts and fast
solutions- but often what I need is more of their
antithesis.

So I sit and listen to immobile nature being
composed as if it were a movement of music.
And I try to learn from the waiting of winter.

Look to the Light

Enveloped by shadows,
Dreary the night seems,
And everlasting,
As if the stars themselves refused to gleam.

But in the dimness
I strike a match,
I fan the flame,
And remind myself that light can yet remain.

Sometimes my mind seems intent to in the
darkness lie
And on repeat the times I've spent in sadness
wither by.
Entrapped by these lonely feelings,
How to keep my mind from reeling?
I try to remember that even the blackest
midnight is only a precursor to light.

Just as in nature the day, too, takes its turn.
And love emerges from the gloom which may
have made me blind.
Even when we cannot see it,
Boldly the coming good still sits
Waiting to catch the gleam in our eyes.
For we are of the stars, and we will still shine.

Leaving

From a young age I felt tortured by the idea of
people walking away
Childhood friends who had to move,
Who I would have gone with if I could choose.
Instead I was left behind,
And it felt like I was the loser.
Several years down the line
When my depression wanted to swallow me
whole,
I took a look around me and decided
Maybe it would be best for me to go.

But can you ever really leave yourself?

Now, today, sitting here
Blinking through my tears
I'm grateful I didn't abandon
That version of me that felt lost and alone.
And that in ways big and small
I have been spent many hard won days
Proving that life is worth sticking around for.

Staying

If I sent an invitation for a party
Ten years from today,

And asked for your RSVP-
What would you say?

There is truly no way of knowing
Where any of us will be.

So maybe staying is not
As cut and dry as I think.

I have been so lucky to have
Friends who have stood by me

While not being physically
Beside me at all.

Sometimes my greatest struggles
Come from wanting to do it all on my own.

But they don't hold it against me,
They are steady, my rocks,

The pillars

I can lean on,

And in turn
They can rely on me.

For the friends who remain,
A thanks doesn't feel like enough.

I know when I am feeling blue
My focus can be rough.

It might seem like I only see
The hurt, the betrayal, the negative voices.

But you remain constant,
And I know it is a conscious choice.

You do not have to stick around
For all the ups and downs.

Yet here you are.

Thank you
For staying.

More Than Picture Perfect

Chase the sunsets,
Chase the moon,

Chase the beauties that seem fleeting,
Gone too soon.

There may never be another sky
Quite like the one you saw today.

Sometimes we have to stop, look up,
And let our breath be taken away.

A picture can preserve the memory,
But don't forget to let your eyes, also, see.

I heard once, "a camera could never do justice
To sunrises or sunsets, to you or me."

Certain sights are not meant to be contained
Inside a rectangular photo frame.

There are lights you cannot begin to capture,
And there are colors you cannot name.

But preserved in photo or memory,

There are visions that can be life-changing.

So chase after those particular rare views,
They'll be worth the schedule rearranging.

Vicious Cycle

How often do I let a good day
Descend into the negativity of my anxiety
riddled brain?

I know I am more than these
Harsh patterns of thought,
These downward spirals that leave me
Drained and empty.

Deep down I feel the stirring
Of a truth on my heart impressed
That I am far more than my latest mistake,
That my worth is not based on pass or fail tests.

Still I harbor guilts and blame myself
For every ill-fated moment,
Trying for accountability,
But just ending up emotional spent.

There does not always have to be a scapegoat,
The blame is not always on my shoulders.
But yet I keep placing it there,
The shame as heavy as boulders.

Falling, weighing, pulling me down-
When will the cycle be over?

apricots

Few things can take me back in time
So fast as a soft pinkish-orange shade-
A color I can practically taste-
Or the offering of a juicy red tomato
(In front of me they'll never go to waste).
Even though I struggle to eat it from the cob, an
ear of corn always delights me
Because of how it reminds me
Of the "hobby" both of my grandpas
Worked at like a full-time job!
It was rare to make a visit
Without seeing them out in it,
Those rows of fruits and veggies
They tended to almost religiously.
And now seeing fresh produce
Can make me want to cry.
I miss those remarkable gardens,
But moreso I miss the men
That made all places magical
Just by stepping foot in them.
It's been years but still I wonder
If they could see me now
What spell they'd think me under
When an apple or cucumber
Leaves me frozen in place?

Do they know their legacies?
And how in my heart a garden grows
Full of the sweetest memories,
Flavored sometimes with sadness
That the greatest gardeners I have known
Won't now be walking through these grasses.

Shooting Stars Do Not Fall Idly

When was the last time that you really dreamed?
When was the last time that you dared
To wrench from the skies
A possibility yet unrealized-
Peeling back the guise
That you don't deserve it?
Reminding yourself, instead,
That you are worth it.
Worth rending the opportunities you want right
from the heavens.

Is it a Curse to Feel So Deeply?

Wrapped in regret,
Lingering in loneliness,
Feeling forgotten in failure--
As if only outward success
Can be the measuring
Tool of my worth.

Languid in laziness,
I feel the depression drain me,
My motivation miserably melting away.
Leaving me draped in the despair of another
wasted day.

Ruinous rage,
Anger aims its arrows
At wrongs I cannot change
Until I'm left withering in under the
Weight of my supposed worthlessness.

I try to trap and tame these feelings,
To smother the sentiments
That so often bring tears to my eyes.
But I'm learning not to stamp out the sensations

Attempting to teach me that my passions do not
need to be put down.

27

New Skin

The funny thing about snakes is they don't start
shedding their skin and then pump the breaks
and think, "Wait, that old look was comfortable,
let me crawl back in!" They let the past be, and
look back on what they outgrew without envy.

And while they are rather sly creatures, I doubt
they waste time comparing their features. They
don't lie in wait for another snake to leave
behind its skin and then clamber in! It just
wouldn't fit, it couldn't be right. Some part
would be too big, another too tight.

The reality is that our bodies aren't meant to fit
on one another, and while we should admire and
enjoy each unique design, the layout doesn't
need to be copied, it's suits each individual just
fine. Each outline, each curve, every line and
bone is in a place that is just its own.

Stop trying to squeeze into or hide
Under layers that were never meant for you.
Let yourself grow out of old thoughts and ideas
Into something brand new.

Choosing Sides

A long-standing war
Wages in my mind.
One side belittles my character,
Leaves me exposed, maligned,
Made out to be
Only the worst parts of me.
Cries of, "nothing here to save,"
Want to drive me to an early grave.

Another side, that often seems
To be stuck as the losing team,
Refuses to be silenced,
Fortified by hope and dreams.
While there is still an awareness of flaws,
I am accepted as I am, vulnerable and raw.
With my humanness laid bare,
A different type of power declares,
"You do not have to be the best,
For even when you are a mess
You can see that value lies
Within the heart that keeps you alive."

One side screams that your worth must be
earned,

The other gently reminds you of the love that
you have learned,
Love that takes time,
Fighting through self-sabotage like grime.
And while it may not be the easy thing to do,
I know which side I want to fight for-- do you?

www.ingramcontent.com/pod-product-compliance
Lightning Source LLC
LaVergne TN
LVHW010933200726
843509LV00013B/2194

Canvassing Art

V. Shruti Devi

BookLeaf Publishing

India | USA | UK

Canvassing Art © 2024 V. Shruti Devi

All rights reserved.

The poet (author) V. Shruti Devi, holds all copyrights over this book, Canvassing Art.

The manuscript and the final manuscript are the exclusive property of V. Shruti Devi

This is the First Edition of the book.

The publishers have the author's permission to non-exclusively use the author's final manuscript and paintings to publish and to exclusively sell the First Edition of Canvassing Art as page-designed by BookLeaf Publishing.

All the paintings showcased in the book are by the poet, V. Shruti Devi, who holds all rights over the said paintings.

V. Shruti Devi asserts the moral right to be identified as the author of this work.

Presentation by *BookLeaf Publishing*, (Co-ordination with V. Shruti Devi by Arushi and Roosha of BookLeaf Publishing)

Book cover design by Hemapriya and Mujtaba Feroz Shah, BookLeaf Design Team in consultation with V. Shruti Devi

Web: www.bookleafpub.com

E-mail: info@bookleafpub.com

ISBN: 9789363309128

First Edition 2024